Milk for Little Ones

An Introduction to the Baptist Catechism

Ryan C. Hodson

The Institute of Reformed Baptist Studies
Printed by RBAP, Palmdale, CA

Requests for information should be sent to:

RBAP
349 Sunrise Terrace
Palmdale, CA 93551
rb@rbap.net
www.rbap.net

Printed in the United States of America.

Cover design and formatted for print by Sean Saclolo.

ISBN-13: 978-0-9965198-6-1

This catechism is dedicated to my son,

Carlos.

May you flee to Christ

and find rest for your soul in his promises.

Table of Contents

Series Preface 1

Acknowledgements 5

1. Creation 11

2. The Godhead 13

3. The Bible 17

4. Man 19

5. The Covenant of Works 21

6. Sin 23

7. The Covenant of Grace 29

8. Repentance and Faith 35

9. The Establishment of the Covenant of

    Grace 37

10. The Offices of Christ 41

11. The Ten Commandments 45

12. The Lord's Prayer 55

13. The Church 61

14. The Last Judgment and the World to Come 67

For Further Reading 71

Series Preface

The purpose of the series *Recovering our Confessional Heritage* is to address issues related to the Second London Confession of Faith of 1677/89 (2LCF). This centuries-old Confession is widely recognized as the most important Confession of Faith in Baptist history. First published in England in 1677, it became the standard for Baptists in Colonial America through the publication of the Philadelphia (1742), Ketockton, Virginia (1766), Charleston, South Carolina, Warren, Rhode Island (both 1767), and many other editions of the Confession. As late as 1881, William Cathcart, the editor of *The Baptist Encyclopedia*, could say, "In England and America, churches, individuals, and Associations, with clear minds, with hearts full of love for the truth, . . . have held with veneration the articles of 1689." Since then, it has been adopted by Baptists around the world and translated into many languages.

We believe that, due to two factors, producing a series of short books on the 2LCF will be useful to many pastors and church members. First, there has been increased interest in the 2LCF in the first decade and a half of the twenty-first century. In fact, from the early 1960s, a greater awareness of this Confession among Baptists in the United States and around the world is evident. One of the encouraging proofs of this growing attention is the multiplication of churches who identify the 2LCF as their confessional standard.

Second, there are many issues related to the Confession that need to be clearly and cogently explained in order for an informed and robust recovery of Baptist confessionalism to continue. While churches and individuals have formally adopted the 2LCF as a standard, it has not always been clear that its contents have been fully or properly understood. As a result, the goal of this series is to aid those considering the 2LCF, as well as those already committed to it, in order to produce or maintain an informed and vigorous Baptist confessionalism.

The series will include treatments of various subjects by multiple authors. The subjects to be covered are those the series editors (along with consultants) determine to be of particular interest in our day. The authors will be those who display ample ability to address the issue under discussion. Some of the installments will be more involved than others due to the nature of the subject addressed and perceived current needs. Many of the contributions will cover foundational aspects of the self-consistent theological system expressed in the Confession. Others will address difficult, often misunderstood, or even denied facets of the doctrinal formulations of the 2LCF. Each installment will have a "For Further Reading" bibliography at the end to encourage further study on the issue discussed.

It is hoped that, by the blessing of God, these brief books will produce a better understanding of "the faith which was once for all delivered to the saints" (Jude 3, NKJV) as well as a clearer and more robust understanding of what it means to confess the 2LCF in the twenty-first century.

James M. Renihan, Editor-in-Chief
Richard C. Barcellos, Managing Editor

October 2016

Acknowledgements

This catechism is largely adapted from the nineteenth-century American Presbyterian catechism titled *Catechism for Young Children: Being an Introduction to the Shorter Catechism*, written by Joseph P. Engels. I have tried to follow closely the original catechism where theologically and stylistically optimal.

There are two other modern-day adaptations of the original—*A Catechism for Boys and Girls*, by Carey Publications of Reformation Today Trust, and *First Catechism* by Great Commission Publications. At times, I chose to follow in the footsteps of these two modern versions for purposes of modernization, theology, or greater clarity. I give my sincerest thanks to the Board of Trustees of Reformation Today Trust, as well as Great Commission Publications, for their generous permission to use some of their copyrighted material.

As to the reason for writing this catechism, while there are many excellent Reformed Baptist catechisms available today, I desired to have one that was not only a bit more robust in its exposition of covenant theology, but which also explicitly outlined the particular type of covenant theology to which I hold, namely 1689 Federalism.

As to the use of this catechism, it should be noted that Engels's catechism was intended as an introduction to the Westminster *Shorter Catechism*. The Baptist equivalent of the Westminster *Shorter Catechism* is the *Baptist Catechism*, also known as *Keach's Catechism*, which was itself a Baptist adaptation of the *Shorter Catechism*. Therefore, this catechism which you hold in your hands is intended to be an introduction to the *Baptist Catechism*. It should be used by parents, Sunday School teachers, and pastors to instruct the very youngest of children in the basics of the Christian religion and to prepare them for catechesis in the *Baptist Catechism* once a good foundation has been laid.

May we earnestly heed the call to catechize our children, especially in the days in which we find ourselves. Our Particular Baptist forebears were keenly aware of the vital role that catechizing played in discipling the next generation of the church. They gave a sobering rebuke in the preface of the *Second London Confession of Faith*:

And verily there is one spring and cause of the decay of religion in our day, which we cannot but touch upon, and earnestly urge a redress of; and that is the neglect of the worship of God in families, by those to whom the charge and conduct of them is committed. May not the gross ignorance, and instability of many; with the prophaneness of others, be justly charged upon their parents and masters who have not trained them up in the way wherein they ought to walk when they were young? But have neglected those frequent and solemn commands which the Lord hath laid upon them so to catechize, and instruct them, that their tender years might be seasoned with the knowledge of the truth of God as revealed in the scriptures; and also by their own omission of prayer, and other duties of religion in their families, together with the ill example of their loose conversation, have inured them first to a neglect, and then contempt of all piety and religion? We know this will not excuse the blindness, or wickedness of any; but certainly it will fall heavy upon those that have thus been the occasion thereof; they indeed die in their sins; but will not their blood be required of those under whose care they were, who yet permitted them to go on without warning, yea, led them into the paths of destruction? And will not the diligence of Christians with respect to the discharge of these duties, in ages past, rise up in judgment against, and condemn many of those who would be esteemed such now?

May we heed the call which is given to every generation of believers: to train up our children in the fear and admonition of the Lord.

Lastly, I would like to acknowledge my appreciation and indebtedness to the following people: to my loving wife, Anika, for all her support and encouragement; to the saints of Sovereign Joy Reformed Baptist Church, who have made pastoring a joyful, light burden; to Jim Renihan for his encouragement and guidance; to Richard Barcellos and Sam Renihan for their invaluable pastoral and theological input into this catechism; and last, but not at all least, the Lord Jesus Christ, who loved us and gave himself up for us! May he use this catechism for his kingdom and in bringing many sons and daughters to glory. Amen!

Ryan C. Hodson, Pastor
Sovereign Joy Reformed Baptist Church
Haltom City, TX
December 2020

1.
Creation

Q. 1. Who made you?

A. God.
Genesis 1:26–27; Psalm 100:3

Q. 2. Where did God make you?

A. God made me in my mother's womb.
Job 31:15; Psalm 139:13

Q. 3. What else did God make?

A. God made all things.
Genesis 1; John 1:3

Q. 4. Why did God make you and all things?

A. For his own glory.
Psalm 66:4; Isaiah 43:7; Revelation 4:11

Q. 5. How can you glorify God?

A. By loving him and doing what he commands.
Ecclesiastes 12:13; Micah 6:8; John 14:15, 21

Q. 6. Why ought you to glorify God?

A. Because he made me and takes care of me.
Psalm 139:14; Psalm 145:9–10; Luke 12:28

Creation

2.
The Godhead

Q. 7. What is God?

A. God is Spirit and does not have a body like we do.
John 4:24; 1 Timothy 1:17

Q. 8. Where is God?

A. God is everywhere.
Psalm 139:7–10; Jeremiah 23:23–24

Q. 9. Can you see God?

A. No. I cannot see God, but he always sees me.
Psalm 33:13–15; Proverbs 5:21; Colossians 1:15

Q. 10. Does God know all things?

A. Yes. Nothing can be hidden from him.
Psalm 139:1–4; Luke 12:7; Hebrews 4:13

Q. 11. Can God do all things?

A. Yes. God can do all his holy will.
Jeremiah 32:17; Luke 1:37; Ephesians 1:11

Q. 12. How many gods are there?

A. There is only one true and living God.
Deuteronomy 6:4; Jeremiah 10:1–5; 1
Corinthians 8:5–6

Q. 13. In how many persons does this one God
exist?

A. In three persons.
Matthew 3:16–17; 2 Corinthians 13:14

The Godhead

Q. 14. What are their names?

A. The Father, the Son, and the Holy Spirit.
Matthew 28:19

The Godhead

3.

The Bible

Q. 15. Where do you learn how to love and obey God?

A. In the Bible, God's word.
Psalm 1; 119:9–11

Q. 16. Who wrote the Bible?

A. Holy men who were guided by the Holy Spirit.
Acts 1:16; 2 Timothy 3:15–16; 2 Peter 1:21

4.
Man

Q. 17. Who were our first parents?

A. Adam and Eve.
Genesis 2:18–23; 3:20

Q. 18. Of what were our first parents made?

A. God made the body of Adam out of the ground and formed Eve from Adam's body.
Genesis 2:7; 2:21–23

Q. 19. What did God give Adam and Eve besides bodies?

A. He gave them souls that could never die.
Genesis 2:7; Matthew 10:28

Q. 20. Do you have a soul as well as a body?

A. Yes. I have a soul that can never die.
Ecclesiastes 12:7; Philippians 1:22–24;
James 2:26

Q. 21. How do you know that you have a soul?

A. Because God has written his law in my heart
and given me a conscience.
Romans 2:14–15; 9:1

Q. 22. In what condition did God make Adam
and Eve?

A. He made them holy and happy.
Genesis 1:27; 1:31; Ecclesiastes 7:29

Man

5.

The Covenant of Works

Q. 23. What is a covenant?

A. A binding commitment between two or more persons.
Genesis 9:12; 26:28–29; Jeremiah 31:31–34

Q. 24. What covenant did God make with Adam?

A. The covenant of works.
Genesis 2:15–17; Hosea 6:7

Q. 25. What did God require of Adam in the covenant of works?

A. To obey God perfectly.
Genesis 1:28

Q. 26. What did God promise in the covenant of works?

A. To reward Adam with eternal life if he obeyed God perfectly.
Genesis 3:22; Leviticus 18:5

Q. 27. What did God threaten in the covenant of works?

A. To punish Adam with death if he disobeyed.
Genesis 2:17

Q. 28. Did Adam keep the covenant of works?

A. No. He sinned against God.
Genesis 3:1–6; Hosea 6:7; Romans 5:12

6.
Sin

Q. 29. What is sin?

A. Sin is any lack of conformity to, or transgression of, the law of God.
1 John 3:4; James 2:9

Q. 30. What does lack of conformity mean?

A. Not being or doing what God requires.
1 Samuel 12:23; Matthew 23:23

Q. 31. What does transgression mean?

A. Doing what God forbids.
Joshua 23:16; Romans 4:15

Q. 32. What does every sin deserve?

A. The wrath and curse of God.
Romans 1:18; Deuteronomy 27:26

Q. 33. What was the sin of our first parents?

A. Eating the forbidden fruit.
Genesis 3:6

Q. 34. Who tempted Adam and Eve to this sin?

A. The devil tempted Eve, and she gave the fruit to Adam.
Genesis 3:1-6

Q. 35. What happened to Adam and Eve when they sinned?

A. Instead of being holy and happy, they became sinful and miserable.
Genesis 3:7, 10; 3:16–19

Q. 36. Did Adam act only for himself in the covenant of works?

A. No. He represented all mankind.
Romans 5:12; 1 Corinthians 15:22

Q. 37. What effect did the sin of Adam have on all mankind?

A. All mankind is born in a state of sin and misery.
Genesis 6:5; Ecclesiastes 7:20; Ephesians 2:3

Q. 38. Are you also then born in a state of sin and misery?

A. Yes. I too was born a sinner and stand guilty before a holy God, and I cannot avoid God's curse by my own deeds.
Psalm 51:5; Romans 3:10, 23; Galatians 2:16

Q. 39. What is that sinful nature which we inherit from Adam called?

A. Original sin.
Romans 5:15; 1 Corinthians 15:22

Q. 40. Can you go to heaven with this sinful nature?

A. No. My heart must be changed before I can go to heaven.
John 3:3; 1 Corinthians 6:9–10

Q. 41. What do we call this change of heart?

A. Regeneration.
Titus 3:5

Q. 42. Who can change your heart?

A. The Holy Spirit alone.
John 3:5; 6:63

Q. 43. Can anyone be saved through the covenant of works?

A. No one can be saved through the covenant of works.
Romans 3:20; Galatians 3:21

Sin

Q. 44. Why can no one be saved through the covenant of works?

A. Because all have broken it in Adam and are condemned by it.
Romans 5:18–19

7.
The Covenant of Grace

Q. 45. How then can you be saved?

A. By the Lord Jesus Christ through the covenant of grace.
Acts 4:11–12; Hebrews 9:15

Q. 46. What is the covenant of grace?

A. God's merciful covenant whereby he promises to freely pardon the sins of all who trust in Christ and to give them new hearts and eternal life.

Q. 47. Who is the head and mediator of the covenant of grace?

A. Jesus Christ.

1 Timothy 2:5-6; Hebrews 9:15; 12:24

Q. 48. What is a mediator?

A. Someone who represents others before God and acts on their behalf.
Hebrews 5:1; 9:24; 1 Peter 3:18

Q. 49. What has Christ done for his people in the covenant of grace as their mediator?

A. He kept the whole law that they could not keep and suffered the punishment their sins deserve.
Romans 5:6–8; 8:3-4; 2 Corinthians 5:21; Galatians 3:13–14

Q. 50. Did our Lord Jesus ever commit even the least sin?

A. No. He lived a perfectly holy life.
Hebrews 4:15; 7:26; 1 Peter 2:22

Q. 51. What kind of life did Christ live on earth?

A. A life of obedience and suffering.
Isaiah 53:3; Matthew 26:39; Hebrews 5:7–8

Q. 52. What kind of death did Jesus die?

A. The painful and shameful death of the cross.
John 19:16–18; Galatians 3:13; Hebrews 12:2

Q. 53. How could the Son of God suffer?

A. Christ, the Son of God, became a man that he might obey and suffer in our nature.
John 1:14; Philippians 2:5–8

Q. 54. What is meant by the atonement?

A. Christ's satisfying God's justice, by his sufferings and death, in the place of sinners.
Isaiah 53:5; Romans 5:8; 2 Corinthians 5:21

Q. 55. What happened to Jesus after he died?

A. His body was wrapped in a linen shroud and placed in a tomb, which was sealed with a large stone.
Matthew 27:57–60; Mark 15:45–46;
Luke 23:50–53

Q. 56. Did Jesus remain in the tomb?

A. No. He rose from the tomb on the third day after his death.
Matthew 28:5–7; Mark 16:4–7; Luke 24:1–9

Q. 57. Where is Jesus now?

A. In heaven, where he sits on his throne and intercedes for sinners.
Isaiah 53:12; Romans 8:34; Hebrews 7:25; 8:1

Q. 58. Will he come again?

A. Yes. He will come again to gather his saints and judge the living and the dead.
Matthew 26:63–64; 2 Thessalonians 1:6–10;
Revelation 22:12

The Covenant of Grace

Q. 59. What benefits does God promise to us in the covenant of grace?

A. To justify and sanctify those for whom Christ died.
Jeremiah 31:33–34; 1 Corinthians 1:30; 6:11

Q. 60. What is justification?

A. It is God's freely forgiving sinners and treating them as if they had lived a perfectly sinless life like Jesus.
Genesis 15:6; Romans 4:5–8; Philippians 3:8–9

Q. 61. What is sanctification?

A. It is God's causing sinners to grow in holiness of heart and conduct.
Ephesians 5:25–27; Philippians 2:12–13; 1 Thessalonians 5:23

8.
Repentance and Faith

Q. 62. What must you do in order to be saved?

A. Repent of my sin and believe in Jesus.
Acts 2:21; 3:19; 16:30–31; Romans 10:9–10

Q. 63. What is it to repent?

A. To be sorry for my sin, and to hate and forsake it because it is displeasing to God.
Isaiah 6:5; Luke 3:10–14; 2 Corinthians 7:9–11; Ephesians 4:28

Q. 64. What is it to believe or have faith in Christ?

A. To trust in Jesus alone for salvation.
John 1:12; 2 Timothy 1:12; Hebrews 11:1, 13

Q. 65. Can you repent and believe in Jesus by your own power?

A. No. I can do nothing good without the help of God's Holy Spirit.
John 3:5–8; 6:63; 1 Corinthians 2:13–14

Q. 66. How can you get the help of the Holy Spirit?

A. God has told us that we must pray to him for the Holy Spirit.
Ephesians 3:16

Q. 67. How long ago is it since Jesus lived and died on the earth?

A. More than two thousand years.
Luke 2:1–2; Acts 4:27

Repentance and Faith

9.
The Establishment
of The Covenant of Grace

Q. 68. When did God first reveal the covenant of grace?

A. God first revealed the covenant of grace to Adam and Eve in the promise of a savior.
Genesis 3:15

Q. 69. When did God officially establish the covenant of grace?

A. God officially established the covenant of grace with the blood of Christ in the new covenant.
Jeremiah 31:31; Hebrews 8:6; 9:15–18

Q. 70. Why was the blood of Christ necessary to officially establish the covenant of grace?

A. Because a death had to occur in order for the covenant to be established, just as the old covenant of Moses was established with the death and blood of calves and goats.
Hebrews 9:15–18

Q. 71. But did the covenant of grace exist before the new covenant in Christ?

A. Yes. The substance of the covenant of grace, with all its benefits, existed before the new covenant in the promise of a savior and has always been the same.
Galatians 3:8, 18

Q. 72. How were people saved before the establishment of the covenant of grace in the coming of Christ?

A. By believing in the promise of the savior to come.
Genesis 15:6; John 8:56

Q. 73. How did they show their faith?

A. By trusting God and obeying his word.
Hebrews 11

10.
The Offices of Christ

Q. 74. What is meant by office?

A. An office is a way of serving God and others by performing certain duties.

Q. 75. How many offices does Jesus have as mediator of the covenant of grace?

A. Three.

Q. 76. What are they?

A. The offices of prophet, priest, and king.

Q. 77. How is Christ a prophet?

A. Because he teaches us the will of God.
Deuteronomy 18:15; Luke 4:24; 24:19

Q. 78. Why do you need Christ as a prophet?

A. Because I am ignorant.
Ephesians 5:17; 1 Corinthians 3:1–3; Hebrews 5:11–14

Q. 79. How is Christ a priest?

A. Because he died for our sins and prays to God for us.
Isaiah 53:12; Romans 8:34; Hebrews 7:25; 9:11–12; 10:11–12

Q. 80. Why do you need Christ as a priest?

A. Because I am guilty.
Psalm 25:11; James 2:10

The Offices of Christ

Q. 81. How is Christ a king?

A. Because he rules over us and defends us.
Luke 1:32–33; Romans 16:20; 2 Thessalonians 1:6–10

Q. 82. Why do you need Christ as a king?

A. Because I am weak and helpless.
Mark 14:38; Hebrews 12:12–13

11.
The Ten Commandments

Q. 83. How many commandments did God give on Mount Sinai?

A. Ten Commandments.
Exodus 34:28

Q. 84. What are the ten commandments sometimes called?

A. The Decalogue, or ten words.

Q. 85. What do the first four commandments teach?

A. Our duty to God.
Exodus 20:1–11; Deuteronomy 5:6–15

Q. 86. What do the last six commandments teach?

A. Our duty to our neighbor.
Exodus 20:12–17; Deuteronomy 5:16–21

Q. 87. What is the sum of the ten commandments?

A. To love God with all my heart, and my neighbor as myself.
Matthew 22:35–40

Q. 88. Who is your neighbor?

A. Everyone is my neighbor.
Luke 10:29–37

Q. 89. Is God pleased with those who love and obey him?

A. Yes. He says, "I love those who love me."
Proverbs 8:17; 15:9

The Ten Commandments

Q. 90. Is God displeased with those who do not love and obey him?

A. Yes. God is indignant every day towards the wicked.
Psalm 7:11; 11:5

Q. 91. What is the first commandment?

A. The first commandment is: "You shall have no other gods before me."
Exodus 20:3; Deuteronomy 5:7

Q. 92. What does the first commandment teach us?

A. To worship God alone.
Deuteronomy 6:13–15; Luke 4:8

Q. 93. What is the second commandment?

A. The second commandment is: "You shall not make for yourself a carved image, or any likeness of anything that is in heaven above, or that is in the earth beneath, or that is in the

water under the earth. You shall not bow down to them or serve them, for I the LORD your God am a jealous God, visiting the iniquity of the fathers on the children to the third and the fourth generation of those who hate me, but showing steadfast love to thousands of those who love me and keep my commandments."
Exodus 20:4–6; Deuteronomy 5:8–10

Q. 94. What does the second commandment teach us?

A. To worship God only as he commands and to not make images or pictures of God.
Exodus 25:9; Leviticus 10:1–2; Romans 1:22–23

Q. 95. What is the third commandment?

A. The third commandment is: "You shall not take the name of the LORD your God in vain, for the LORD will not hold him guiltless who takes his name in vain."
Exodus 20:7; Deuteronomy 5:11

Q. 96. What does the third commandment teach us?

A. To honor and cherish God's name, word, and works.
Psalm 111:2–7; 113:1–3; 138:2

Q. 97. What is the fourth commandment?

A. "Remember the Sabbath day, to keep it holy. Six days you shall labor, and do all your work, but the seventh day is a Sabbath to the LORD your God. On it you shall not do any work, you, or your son, or your daughter, your male servant, or your female servant, or your livestock, or the sojourner who is within your gates. For in six days the LORD made heaven and earth, the sea, and all that is in them, and rested on the seventh day. Therefore the LORD blessed the Sabbath day and made it holy."
Exodus 20:8–11; Deuteronomy 5:12–15

Q. 98. What does the fourth commandment teach us?

A. To keep the Sabbath holy.
Isaiah 58:13–14

Q. 99. What day of the week is the Christian Sabbath?

A. The first day of the week, called the Lord's day.
Acts 20:7; 1 Corinthians 16:2; Revelation 1:10

Q. 100. Why is it called the Lord's day?

A. Because on that day the Lord Jesus rose from the dead.
Matthew 28:1-7; Mark 16:1-7; Luke 24:1-7

Q. 101. How should the Sabbath be kept?

A. In prayer and praise, in hearing and reading God's word, and in doing good to one another.
Matthew 12:11-12; Colossians 3:16; 1 Timothy 4:13

Q. 102. What is the fifth commandment?

A. The fifth commandment is: "Honor your father and your mother, that your days may be

long in the land that the LORD your God is giving you."
Exodus 20:12; Deuteronomy 5:16

Q. 103. What does the fifth commandment teach us?

A. To love and obey our parents and teachers.
Exodus 22:28; Ephesians 6:1–3; Hebrews 13:17

Q. 104. What is the sixth commandment?

A. The sixth commandment is: "You shall not murder."
Exodus 20:13; Deuteronomy 5:17

Q. 105. What does the sixth commandment teach us?

A. To never sin against others with our words or deeds, and to not have unrighteous anger towards anyone.
Matthew 5:21–22; James 4:1–3

Q. 106. What is the seventh commandment?

A. The seventh commandment is: "You shall not commit adultery."
Exodus 20:14; Deuteronomy 5:18

Q. 107. What does the seventh commandment teach us?

A. To be pure in heart, language, and conduct.
Psalm 24:3-4; 1 Timothy 4:12; 1 Peter 2:12

Q. 108. What is the eighth commandment?

A. The eighth commandment is: "You shall not steal."
Exodus 20:15; Deuteronomy 5:19

Q. 109. What does the eighth commandment teach us?

A. To never take something that is not mine, and to work hard.
Proverbs 9:17-18; Ephesians 4:28; 2 Thessalonians 3:10-12

The Ten Commandments

Q. 110. What is the ninth commandment?

A. The ninth commandment is: "You shall not bear false witness against your neighbor."
Exodus 20:16; Deuteronomy 5:20

Q. 111. What does the ninth commandment teach us?

A. To never lie but always tell the truth.
Psalm 34:12–13; Proverbs 20:17; John 14:6

Q. 112. What is the tenth commandment?

A. The tenth commandment is: "You shall not covet your neighbor's house; you shall not covet your neighbor's wife, or his male servant, or his female servant, or his ox, or his donkey, or anything that is your neighbor's."
Exodus 20:17; Deuteronomy 5:21

Q. 113. What does the tenth commandment teach us?

A. To be content with what God has given me, and to praise him in all things.
Job 1:21; Philippians 4:11–13; 1 Timothy 6:6–8

Q. 114. Can anyone keep these ten commandments perfectly?

A. No mere human, since the fall of Adam, ever did or can keep the ten commandments perfectly.
Romans 2:13; James 2:10; 1 John 1:8, 10

Q. 115. Of what use are the ten commandments?

A. They teach us our duty to God and show us our sin and need of a savior.
Romans 7:7; Galatians 3:24; 1 Timothy 1:8–10

12.
The Lord's Prayer

Q. 116. What is prayer?

A. Prayer is thanking God from the heart for all his blessings and asking him for the things which he has promised us.
Philippians 4:6; 1 Timothy 2:1–3; 1 John 5:14–15

Q. 117. In whose name should we pray?

A. Only in the name of Jesus Christ.
John 14:13–14; 16:23–27

Q. 118. What did Jesus give us to teach us how to pray?

A. The Lord's Prayer.
Matthew 6:9–13

Q. 119. What is the Lord's Prayer.

A. "Our Father in heaven, hallowed be your name. Your kingdom come, your will be done, on earth as it is in heaven. Give us this day our daily bread, and forgive us our debts, as we also have forgiven our debtors. And lead us not into temptation, but deliver us from evil" (Matthew 6:9–13).

Q. 120. How many petitions are in the Lord's Prayer?

A. Six.

Q. 121. What is the first petition?

A. "Hallowed be your name."
Matthew 6:9

Q. 122. What do we pray for in the first petition?

A. That God's name may be honored in all the world.
1 Kings 8:41–43; Psalm 113:3; Malachi 1:11

Q. 123. What is the second petition?

A. "Your kingdom come."
Matthew 6:10

Q. 124. What do we pray for in the second petition?

A. That the gospel may be preached in all the world and believed by all people.
Genesis 12:3; Matthew 24:14; Acts 1:8; 13:47

Q. 125. What is the third petition?

A. "Your will be done on earth as it is in heaven."
Matthew 6:10

Q. 126. What do we pray for in the third petition?

A. That we on earth may serve God as the angels do in heaven.
Psalm 103:20; Isaiah 6:1–3; Revelation 5:11–14

Q. 127. What is the fourth petition?

A. "Give us this day our daily bread."
Matthew 6:11

Q. 128. What do we pray for in the fourth petition?

A. That God would provide for all our daily needs.
Genesis 22:14; Psalm 34:10; Matthew 6:31–33

Q. 129. What is the fifth petition?

A. "And forgive us our debts as we also have forgiven our debtors."
Matthew 6:12

Q. 130. What do we pray for in the fifth petition?

A. That God would pardon our sins for Christ's sake and enable us to forgive those who have sinned against us.
1 John 1:9; Colossians 3:12–13

The Lord's Prayer

Q. 131. What is the sixth petition?

A. "And lead us not into temptation but deliver us from evil."
Matthew 6:13

Q. 132. What do we pray for in the sixth petition?

A. That God would keep us from sin and enable us to flee from temptation.
Luke 22:40; 1 Corinthians 10:13; Hebrews 2:18

13.
The Church

Q. 133. What is the universal or catholic church?

A. The universal or catholic church is a holy assembly of true Christian believers, all expecting their salvation in Jesus Christ, being washed by his blood, sanctified and sealed by the Holy Spirit.
1 Corinthians 1:2; Hebrews 12:22–23

Q. 134. What is a local or particular church?

A. It is a congregation of visible saints joined together by covenant, to worship the Lord and walk together in all his commandments and holy ordinances.
Acts 16:5; 1 Corinthians 1:2; 14:33

Q. 135. What do you mean by visible saints?

A. Visible saints are those who profess the faith of the gospel and obedience unto God, and who do not destroy their profession by error or unholiness of life.
Ephesians 1:1; 5:3; Revelation 14:12

Q. 136. How many sacraments has Christ instituted in his church?

A. Two

Q. 137. What is a sacrament?

A. A visible sign given by Christ to confirm and build up the faith of his people.
Luke 22:19–20; 1 Peter 3:21

Q. 138. What are they?

A. Baptism and the Lord's Supper.

The Church

Q. 139. Why did Christ institute these sacraments?

A. To distinguish his disciples from the world, and to comfort and strengthen them.
Matthew 28:19–20; 1 Corinthians 10:16; 11:26

Q. 140. What is baptism?

A. The immersion or dipping of believers into water.
Matthew 3:5–6; Acts 8:36

Q. 141. What does this signify?

A. The believer's union with Christ and participation in his death and life.
Romans 6:3–4; Colossians 2:11–12

Q. 142. In whose name should baptism be administered?

A. In the name of the Father, and of the Son, and of the Holy Spirit.
Matthew 28:19

Q. 143. Who are to be baptized?

A. Only those who profess the faith of the gospel and obedience unto God.
Mark 16:16; Acts 2:41; 8:12; 18:8; Galatians 3:25–27

Q. 144. Should infants be baptized?

A. No.

Q. 145. Why shouldn't infants be baptized?

A. Because Christ neither commanded it, nor can it be found in the word of God either by example or by good and necessary consequence.
Mark 7:8

Q. 146. But does Jesus not love the little children then?

A. Jesus loves all children and desires that they come to him for salvation.
Matthew 19:13–15

The Church

Q. 147. What is the Lord's Supper?

A. The eating of bread and the drinking of wine in remembrance of the sufferings and death of Christ.
1 Corinthians 11:26

Q. 148. What does the bread represent?

A. The body of Christ, broken for our sins.
Matthew 26:26; Mark 14:22; Luke 22:19

Q. 149. What does the wine represent?

A. The blood of Christ, shed for the forgiveness of sins.
Matthew 26:27–28; Mark 14:23–24; Luke 22:20

Q. 150. Who should partake of the Lord's Supper?

A. Only those who profess the faith of the gospel and obedience unto God, and have been baptized.
Acts 2:41–42; 1 Corinthians 11:26–29

14.
The Last Judgment and The World to Come

Q. 151. What happens to believers when they die?

A. Their bodies return to the dust, and their souls go to be with Jesus.
Ecclesiastes 12:7; Luke 23:43; Philippians 1:23–24

Q. 152. What happens to unbelievers when they die?

A. Their bodies return to the dust, but their souls go to hell.
Genesis 3:19; Psalm 90:3; Luke 16:22–26

Q. 153. Will the bodies of the dead be raised to life again?

A. Yes. Some to everlasting life and others to everlasting death.
Matthew 25:31–46; Acts 24:15

Q. 154. What will happen to believers in the day of judgment?

A. They shall go into everlasting life and receive fullness of joy and glory with everlasting rewards, in the presence of the Lord in the new heavens and the new earth.
Matthew 25:31–40; 1 Corinthians 1:7–8; 2 Timothy 4:7–8; Jude 1:24

Q. 155. What are the new heavens and the new earth?

A. A glorious and happy place, where the righteous shall be with the Lord forever.
Isaiah 65:17–25; 2 Peter 3:13; Revelation 21:1–5

Q. 156. What will happen to unbelievers in the day of judgment?

A. They shall be cast aside into everlasting torments in hell, and punished with everlasting destruction, from the presence of the Lord, and from the glory of his power.
Matthew 7:21–23; 25:41–46

Q. 157. What is hell?

A. A place of dreadful and never-ending torment and fire.
Matthew 13:40–42; Mark 9:43; Luke 16:22–28; Revelation 14:9–11

Q. 158. These things all being true, how then ought you to live?

A. I ought to flee to Jesus in faith and repent of my sins.
Isaiah 55:6–7; Matthew 11:28–30; Romans 10:13

For Further Reading

Beddome, Benjamin. *A Scriptural Exposition of the Baptist Catechism*. Birmingham, AL: Solid Ground Christian Books, 2006.

Dickson, David. *Truth's Victory over Error: A Commentary on the Westminster Confession of Faith*, John R. De Witt, editor. Carlisle, PA: Banner of Truth, 2007.

Helopoulos, Jason. *A Neglected Grace: Family Worship in the Christian Home*. Fearn Ross-Shire, Scotland: Christian Focus Publications, 2013.

Johnson, Terry L. *Catechizing Our Children: The Whys and Hows of Teaching the Shorter Catechism Today*. Carlisle, PA: Banner of Truth, 2013.

Meade, Starr. *Training Hearts, Teaching Minds: Family Devotions Based on the Shorter Catechism*. Phillipsburg, NJ: P & R Publications, 2000.

Renihan, James M. *A Toolkit for Confessions: Helps for the study of English Puritan Confessions of Faith*. Palmdale, CA: RBAP, 2017.